GRIGORI GRABOVOI

Published by
EAM Publishing
GRIGORI GRABOVOI®
Copyright © 2023 Dr. Grigori Grabovoi®
ISBN : 9798378976706

Cover © D'har Services Editorial Art in Global Design
D:132238150©S. productions
Translation from Spanish to English by Maria Barajas, BSN, MSOM

GRIGORI GRABOVOI®
© Grabovoi G.P., 2023
The author's original seminar/seminar was held by Grigori Grabovoi © Grabovoi G.P., February 7, 2000

Education System – Serbia: GRIGORI GRABOVOI D.O.O.
The text of the work was first created by Grabovoi Grigori Petrovich during his seminar on February 7, 2000. When creating the seminar, the method of eternal development with exact forecasting of future events was applied. The validation of 100% of the forecasts made by Grabovoi G.P. have been proven by the protocols and testimonials, published in a 3-volume edition "Practice of Control: The Path of Salvation." When creating the text of the seminar, Grabovoi G.P. first had an accurate forecast of future events, and then he created a text that taught everyone eternal development, taking due account of the specific events of the future, which concern each person and the entire World.

All rights reserved. No part of this book may be reproduced in any form without the written permission of the copyright owner.

PRACTICAL GUIDE TO THE EDUCATIONAL SYSTEM OF GRIGORI GRABOVOI

GRIGORI GRABOVOI
February 7, 2000

My education system is based on concentration and the transfer of knowledge for all people, knowledge can be applied, even from before birth, to babies who are in gestation or newborn babies.

This education system can be done by the baby's parents, grandparents or any person who takes care of the baby and wants to do it for the fundamental development of the new being, or for someone who is in a position to do it for themselves or to support a mother who is expecting her baby, or for anyone who needs to reprogram life.

Education is that stimulus that gives you eternal stability. The correct education is stability forever; this is God's idea. Because the Creator created the World, so that all people develop in this world with respect to his idea of Eternity through understanding and knowledge of this world. In other words, education is actually what you receive and see inside and in front of you. Because when you do and perform something, this is at the same time your education. Therefore, if you have considered education as the formation of the event from the point of view of the fundamental level of the World, then you will always have a control instrument, and your education will be based on this system and there will be no unpredictable action components, sudden and unnecessary, which you will not experience and will not be necessary to you.

Therefore, when I speak of education, I mean that this education creates a systematic level of favorable development, a systematic level of optimization of development, when you are in harmony with the World that is in eternal development, by understanding its connections, and also simultaneously developing the World in the direction of Universal happiness and Creation.

You arrive at the action in the future as to an "already" known action. This is how knowledge of the future is generated, knowledge of the future that allows you, firstly, to be prepared to observe some events, and secondly, to control these events. In fact, education is the formation of the true information creation of the future, which will allow you to have the that which you have selected due to your original nature and essence.

And education from the point of view of knowing the fundamental connections, ensures that true individuality that the Creator intrinsically granted us. Education is your individuality.

You receive what the Creator provides you in the form of thought, in the form of information, in the form of development and you see how it is provided it to you according to the education you are using to perceive. You see when and how you are forming yourself in relation to this and you get an integral personality; that true personality that is always in accordance with God's intention.

The individual who receives an adequate education, a harmonious education, an education with the knowledge of the fundamental laws of the World, that person will develop according to the laws given to him by the Creator. In other words, this will be the true development of your personality and the personality of each individual.

And, having considered how the formation of everything in the World takes place, in spiritual and physical terms, from the point of view of the goals of the Creator, you get the true development of information.

You will receive a true knowledge of deep issues that exist in the World, the deep reasons that exist in the World, not only from the point of view of some sciences, not only from the point of view of some relative elements, but from the point of view of view of the ultimate Creator, the only truth for you, from the point of view of every personality, which follows in line with the intention of the Creator, towards the eternal existence, towards eternal life, towards immortality, when immortality is a reflection of the idea of the Creator, a reflection of the true knowledge of the Creator.

In this way, you receive a true and adequate education, based on the fundamental level of knowledge of the World, and therefore on the control of this World, on the level of organization of the World from information, and as such, control from any part of the World, you receive this level, which according to the initial idea, is that of having a free and independent personality, which was given to you by the Creator.

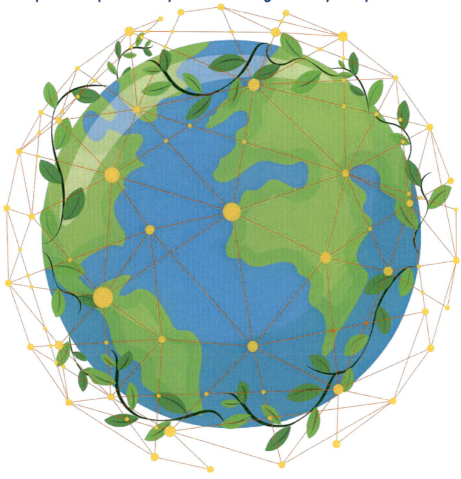

319817318   E=VS

This education system includes several stages.

We are going to start with the education of our being, and we imagine our own mother, being very aware, and who knows how to guide us step by step.

Each one imagines himself/herself as that Soul in formation that will become a great being.

We start with the first stage, which is through concentration on the infinity of time and space before your birth.

Listen:

You are going to be born, and you will develop creatively and you will give eternity to the world.

And concentrate on this first thought:
I am going to be born, and I will develop creatively and I will give eternity to the world.

Now, I guide you mentally from the point at infinity, from the negative infinity $-\infty$ that is on the left and from there to the point of three years, before your birth, visualize the year
_ _ _ _.

1. BEFORE AND AFTER BIRTH

$-\infty$ TO THREE YEARS BEFORE BIRTH

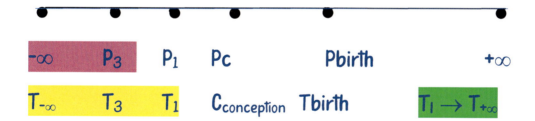

Then you mentally scroll through infinity, you carry this event through reality, which is all the infinite information before your birth.

THROUGH THE $-\infty$ YOU TAKE THIS EVENT THROUGH REALITY

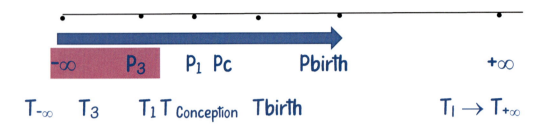

Now that you are already concentrating on that idea, take your thoughts three years before your birth, visualize the year _ _ _ _

And keep in mind the following mental form (create your own mental images):

You will be born, live in happiness, you will be happy and you will be surrounded by love.

Now you concentrate your thought one year before your birth, imagine the year _ _ _ _ .

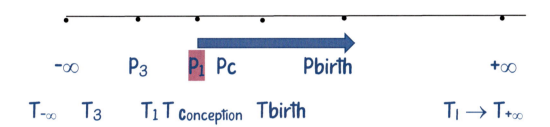

And I tell you:
You are a person who will always be happy and bring happiness and love to others and to yourself. You will always be well supplied with everything you require and need.

You transfer this same thought to infinite information after your birth.

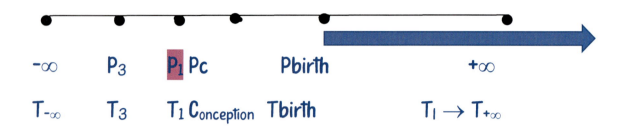

THEN YOU TAKE IT DIRECTLY TO THE POINT OF YOUR BIRTH AND FROM THERE TO THE POINT OF ITS CONCEPTION.

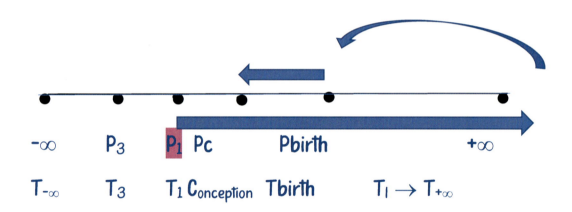

In this way, this action on concentration is carried out a year before your birth and is expressed as movements of your thought along a series of points. Therefore, with these simple and successive actions, it is possible to space these points along a straight line.

CONCEPTION POINT

Then you follow the point of conception (Pc) Which indicates the point of your conception, then you see the point one year before birth – P1, and the point P3 – three years before birth and at negative infinity $-\infty$. And, on the right hand side will be the point of positive infinity $(+)+\infty$.

Therefore, it is necessary to mentally trace from the point of conception; directing the thought to point one and then to point three until negative infinity and then to positive infinity and then to the point of conception:

concentrate on point Pc, the point of conception and from there go to point one, having formulated the thought, which I already told you.

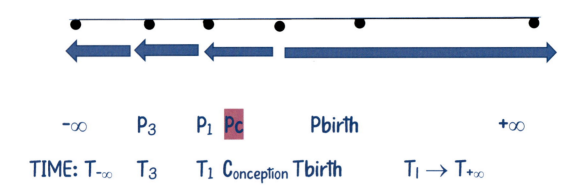

To draw it mentally, it's like you go along the straight line, to aim the Pc (point of conception), next you aim at negative infinity and then at the point of positive infinity and then again go to point Pc.

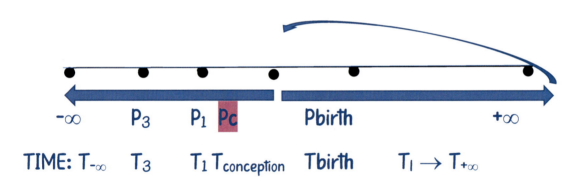

TIME

There is one more point, which is called the birth point, therefore the way it works is the transference occurs like the transfer of the concepts of points in the concept of "TIME," from there, transfer them to the concept Tb, which is the time of birth; Tc is the time of conception; T1, T2, are time one, time two. And it is about T-, which is the time of negative infinity and T+ is the time of positive infinity. So we get a total of four points.

Therefore, these four points indicate the following:

POINT OF BIRTH

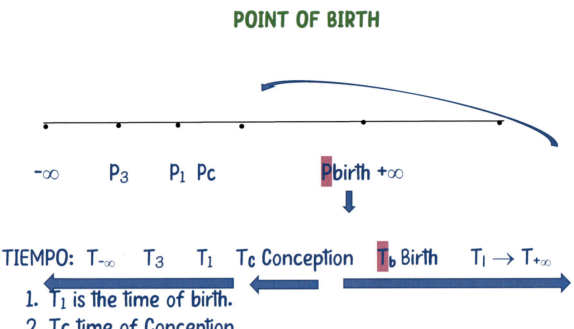

1. T_1 is the time of birth.
2. Tc time of Conception.
3. T- the point of negative infinite time.
4. T+ is the point of positive infinity.

There is also the concept of point, which is the concept of time that I am explaining to you here, and which is the lifetime. Therefore, the lifetime must tend to the moment of infinity. That means, that the meaning of these actions must be expressed in the fact that life becomes infinite, that is, you must tend to positive infinity, therefore, this is no longer indicated by a point, but is an infinite element. Each action, which exists here in this system, is an infinite element, therefore my education system is an infinite element aimed at providing concepts of infinite life, infinite creation, and therefore initially by proceeding with this technology it is developing in exactly this direction.

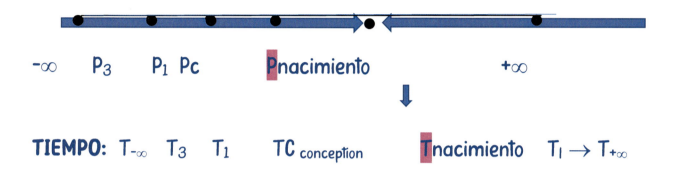

At the same time, all these actions can be carried out with any person, regardless of how old that person is at the moment.

I mean, that it can be used not only for future newborns, but it can also be applied to all people who are already alive; in that case it simply means that these concentrations must be applied to a living person, in order to ensure his development towards infinite life and good health, happiness and love.

So now I'm starting to talk about actions and concentrations, which must be at the point of conception. Therefore, first of all, I am going to introduce the monthly rhythm, from the moment of your conception; and it is for you baby that you are already in this first stage of your development. (During this first month transfer mentally).

It is the scheme of Figure 2, which is also along a straight line, in the interval of the **FIRST MONTH**.

Nine Months of Prenatal Development.

This formula must be transferred mentally: to the fetus, in the **FIRST MONTH** after the time of conception:

   As a baby, you need to focus on trees, animals, and people.

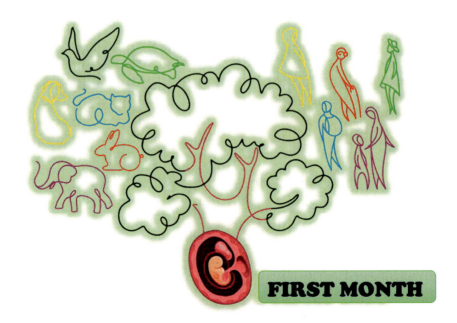

And now that you are in the process of development, I also mentally transmit this law to you:

All the elements of the World and all the particles are connected to each other, and as they connect, they grow.

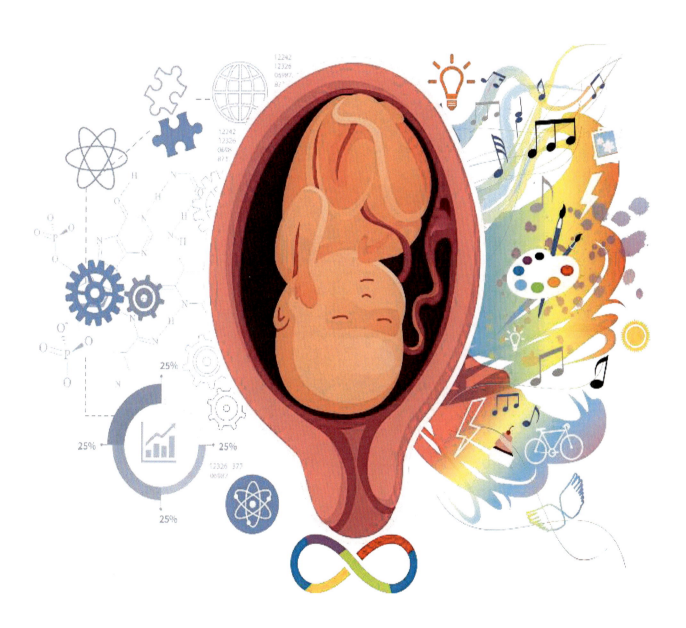

SECOND MONTH OF DEVELOPMENT

 After the point of conception, at the time of actual conception. (During this second month, I transmit to you):

Baby, the world is arranged in such a way that when you think, matter is being organized; and when you are thinking, your affairs will be organized too.

SECOND MONTH

THIRD MONTH OF DEVELOPMENT

 After the moment of conception: (it is necessary to mentally transfer this knowledge throughout the month):

As a Baby, you are part of the World, and you are also an independent part at the same time and therefore you have to think of yourself as a part of the World independently.

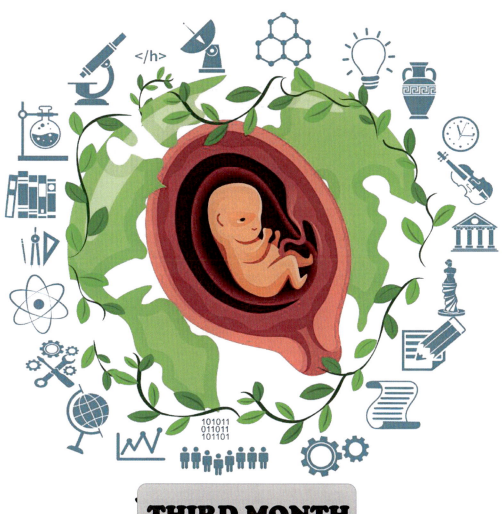

THIRD MONTH

FOURTH MONTH OF DEVELOPMENT

After the moment of conception

(The concept of "periodic transfer" means to mentally cue the fetus, as often as possible, and therefore the more frequently you do it, the better.).

During this fourth month I transmit to you:

As a baby, you are an individual personality, you were already in development from before the moment of conception, you have not appeared from infinity, but you have formed yourself, therefore, your soul and your body are eternal.

FOURTH MONTH

FIFTH MONTH OF DEVELOPMENT

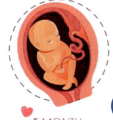

After the moment of conception

(During this fifth month I transmit to you):

Baby, in this current moment, have a clear understanding of how you will develop yourself and the World in a constructive way.

FIFTH MONTH

(Transfer mentally and periodically)

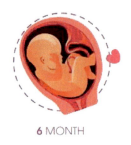

SIXTH MONTH OF DEVELOPMENT

After the moment of conception, during this sixth month, I transmit to you:

(Mentally and periodically transfer the following formula):

As a baby, you are responsible for your parents, for the phenomena in the surrounding world, you yourself construct all events, also understanding that the study of all sciences must take place with consideration of the knowledge that you receive now; all sciences will be transformed in your own mind and will acquire the meaning you give it from the beginning of your development.

SIXTH MONTH

You must understand that infinity, which exists in front of the timeline, will also exist after. This can be combined and transmitted as a mental impulse, as seen in Figure 1 – where you connect the time point of negative infinity ($T_{-\infty}$) to the positive time ($T_{+\infty}$)

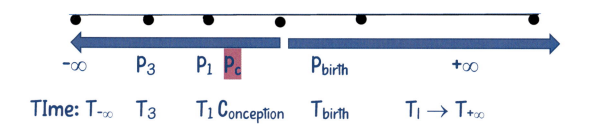

or simply during that sixth month, superimpose the symbol T- «minus» superimposed over T + «plus», and so it turns out that you are already creating life in a harmonized way.

SEVENTH MONTH OF DEVELOPMENT

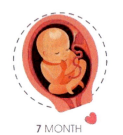

7 MONTH

After the moment of conception during this month, I transmit to you:

Baby, you are responsible for all your actions and you are a person with personality, responsible and mature, in the same way that you were at the moment of conception. Now you must be open, clear and aware, that on the existing basis of the eternal Soul, you can perceive yourself also as a personality developed in that initial moment.

(Periodically transfer mentally the next formula)

SEVENTH MONTH

EIGHTH MONTH OF DEVELOPMENT

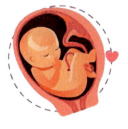

After the moment of conception during this month:

(It is necessary to inform the baby mentally)

You are a person who will be born with the purpose of giving birth to others, creating together with others, resurrecting those who have died before the day of your birth, and not allowing others to die, nor yourself. This is accomplished by having the target at infinity point B (T+).

This is the point ∞ for which you strive and aspire to reach.

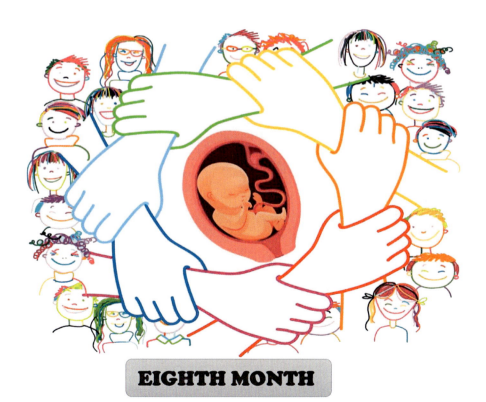

EIGHTH MONTH

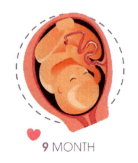

NINETH MONTH OF DEVELOPMENT

After the moment of conception during this month:

(It is necessary to transfer mentally)

You are a person and you will already be able to breathe, move freely and be like others. Now comes the stage of your birth, get used to that moment.

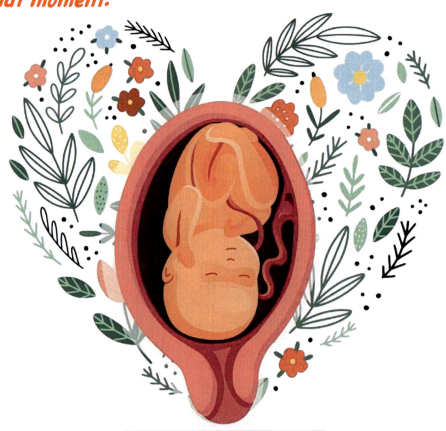

NINETH MONTH

THE NEXT STAGE IS SHOWN IN FIGURE 3

THE MOMENT OF BIRTH

Note: Figure 1 indicates a schematic before birth and Figure 2 is the nine months of fetal development. If the baby has developed and the delivery took place before nine months, the same should still be said as if she was developing at the specific prenatal level. In other words, there is no difference, only in case the baby was born before nine months, superimpose the later time period on top of the current one. For example, suppose the baby was born at seven months, then the subsequent formulas, covering the eighth and ninth months, need to be transmitted at the same time.

Figure 3. Time of birth (period of birth)

AP = Prenatal Period
OAP = Exterior Prenatal Period
EW = The External World

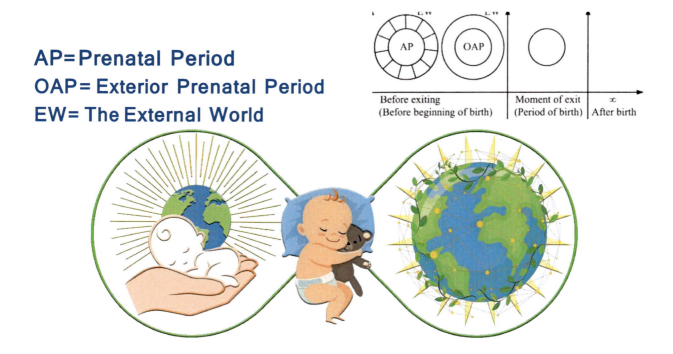

To control this period of moment from the point of view of infinite life, the following actions are required:

Mentally visualize that the baby is connected by infinite connections while in the prenatal period. These are indicated in the figure as AP, the prenatal period appears in the form of a sphere. This sphere has infinite connections that are like small lines, which reach another sphere and this connects the baby to the whole World.

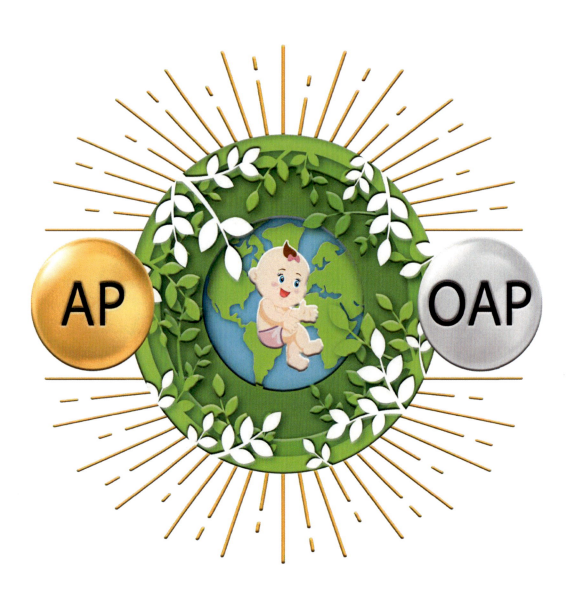

In other words, it is necessary to imagine that there are two spheres. The first sphere is prenatal development and the second is the whole World and there is a connection between them. Therefore, it is necessary to convey very clearly to the person who is born, that prenatal development passes to the next sphere, which is not different the sphere already in place. It changes only in terms of connections with the outer sphere. In other words, it is necessary to convey very clearly that these connections here, which in the form of lines went from the "AP" sphere to the sphere that is termed "OAP," or "outer prenatal period," is when the person has already been born. Therefore the external spheres remain the same, that is what as "EW" – the external World represents.

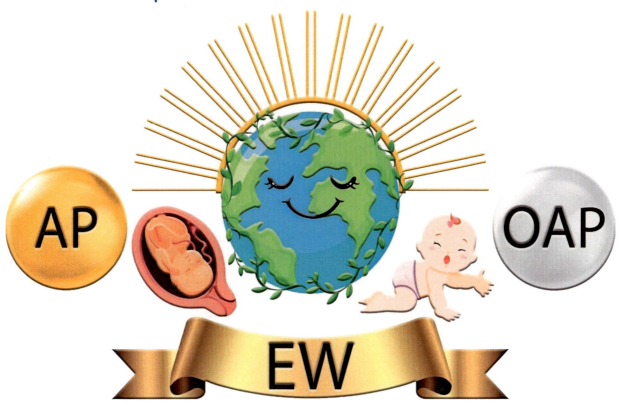

EW" is the external World, this is the external sphere. Clearly imagine that now all lines connecting AP to this sphere are located within the EW sphere, which is the period outside of prenatal development, when the person has already been born. This must be clearly transmitted to the baby before the baby is delivered from the womb at birth. Exactly at that moment, there will be knowledge without any polarized charges (because before the moment of delivery, there appear to be dividing points). Mentally visualize clearly that you deliver the World into his hands, and deliver it to him exactly before the time of departure.

Then the next stage will happen later, i.e. up to positive infinity. Here you have to imagine an infinite open space, which is the infinite plane, the infinite space, and feel that the baby is there, that the baby is in this infinite space. In fact, it seems that you see the baby in that infinite zone.

So those actions that have taken place indicate that:
Baby you are aware of the World before the event occurs and therefore when you combine with awareness therefore you are aiding the birth.

And when you transfer the baby to infinity, then the Baby feels comfortable and normal there.

So, in all of this technology, it's very important to work on it mentally, and as often as possible, it's possible to work on it right up to the time of birth, and for as long as you want.

You can work up to the moment of birth on the area that I have placed in Figure 3.

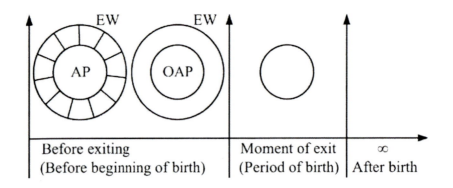

Figure 4. I am showing the transfer of information for the days after birth.

FIGURE 4. INFORMATION FOR THE DAYS AFTER BIRTH (POST-NATAL PERIOD)

FIRST DAY AFTER BIRTH

I transmit to you this idea:

Baby, the World is eternal.

SECOND DAY AFTER BIRTH

Baby, I now transmit to you that the World is constantly changing and simultaneously everything moves as the World develops.

37

THIRD DAY AFTER BIRTH

Baby, you are eternal exactly because you also move and develop.

FOURTH DAY AFTER BIRTH

(Tell the baby several times everything you told him the first three days of his birth).

- Baby, I convey to you the idea that the World is eternal.
- The World is eternal, and at the same time it changes, everything moves and everything in the World develops.
- Baby, you are eternal exactly because you move and develop.

FIFTH DAY AFTER BIRTH

(Ask the baby, mentally):

Baby, mentally transmit to me what you see; how is the World? And how do you understand the world?

When you do this exercise, transmit love and happiness from your Soul, feeling this affection with your loving gaze, give it the opportunity to

delight in all the realities that arise from the juxtaposition of the five planes of the World.
(If you like, you can narrate the information about the planes).

The 5 Planes

Grigori Grabovoi (excerpts from the book): **THE RESURRECTION OF PEOPLE AND ETERNAL LIFE FROM NOW ARE OUR REALITY.**

1 Spiritual Plane: authentic life does not stop; it consists of an uninterrupted development of the spirit, and that is precisely what I want to emphasize in a special way. Spiritual Perfection and spiritual development gives the possibility to see the dynamics of this process, and this, in turn, helps the development of the spiritual structure.

Regarding dimensionality, the following must be taken into account: from the spiritual structure that encompasses all known phenomena, one dimensionality can be transformed into another. Therefore, the concept of the dimensionality of the various spaces is not very important.

Fundamental is the fact that the spiritual structure can be modified, it can be developed, and it is this structure that determines everything else.

I want to warn you: do not under any circumstances think that dimensionality is not fixed once and for all. These dimensionalities have these characteristics today, but tomorrow they may have others.

THERE IS A MUTUAL DEPENDENCE BETWEEN THE SPIRITUAL AND PHYSICAL STRUCTURE, THROUGH THE TRANSFORMATION OF INFORMATION ABOUT THE PHYSICAL STRUCTURE IN THE SPIRIT SPHERE, WE CAN TRANSFORM THE SPIRIT TO A LEVEL WHERE IT CAN MODIFY ANY PHYSICAL STRUCTURE, ACHIEVING THE CREATION OF A PHYSICAL BODY (2.2).

Raising the spirit to the level where it will be able not only to modify a physical structure, but also to create it, and in particular, to create a physical body as well, as a consequence we obtain that man can never die. And if man is capable of not dying, then he himself is also capable of resurrecting others.

2. Mental Plane: The mind is the way to react to information, to action from outside. Since each object can have a reaction to information, to an action from outside,

you can extend the conceptual "mind" of any object. But let's talk about the mind of man. On the other hand, I find it particularly interesting to examine the characteristics of the mind during the development of man.

The mind can be seen as a concept that unites the soul, the spirit, the consciousness, and the body. In the mind, objects are recognized and merged according to their reaction modalities. And thought is that

information that acts as a link between consciousness, spirit, and body; thought is also regulated by the soul.

It is easier to see the mutual relationships between the concepts established here using the example of the following analogy: Imagine a waterfall; the water precipitates under the action of the force of gravity. It can be thought that the force of gravity is compared to the spirit; the water with consciousness; the body corresponds to the riverbed in which the water flows. And the soul corresponds to what created all this, both the Earth, the force of gravity, and the water. In general, the soul participates in creation both directly and through thought.

It can be said that thought is linked to the entire structure of the World and that it represents the concrete action of man in this general structure.

3. Emotional Plane: Life goes on, and naturally, with changing conditions, a new understanding of the development process is born. A NEW STAGE IN THE DEVELOPMENT OF THE PERSON AND SOCIETY.

The question that will now be examined is so serious that it is appropriate to dwell on it in more detail.

Using scientific language, I would have started the discussion by talking about the modification of the paradigm, that is, in the specific case, the change in principle of the behavior model. But I will stay in the context of simple analysis and obvious comparisons.

Let's reflect on how in ancient times, for example, America was reached from Europe. To cross the ocean they used a sailboat. This took a long time. Of course, when you look at the image of a ship with a large

number of sails, you have a very beautiful vision in front of you. But how much time was needed to cross the ocean! And how many dangers awaited a small ship during a storm!
And now instead? Now the situation is very different, if you need to get to the United States more quickly, you can take a plane and after a few hours be at your destination.

Also, take a look at this in detail: now you can get to the United States by sea from Europe and not only faster, but also have greater security and have a greater number of amenities, on a transoceanic line ship there is everything you need: restaurants, dance floors, swimming pools, amenities, etc. everything you could possibly need!

Or, also consider the problem of communications. How long in the past did it take a European to exchange messages with an American acquaintance?

And even without going too far back in history, what was the situation only -for example- in the 19th century? How long did it take between sending a letter and receiving a response? And what is, on the other hand, the current situation?

Today, teleconferences between different countries have become a common phenomenon, and you talk to people who are at the other end of the world and it is as if they were sitting in front of you or their interlocutors. Or, take the World Cup Finals for example. Large numbers of people across the globe are glued to their television screens, watching the game live via satellite link!

Life has changed profoundly. Living conditions have changed. The rhythm of life has become completely different. It is precisely for this reason that the old and slow mechanism of understanding the truths, which developed through the rejection of the physical body, the temporary permanence in another form, in the subtle planes of being, the acquisition in these subtle planes of necessary information, and then the return to the physical body – all this slow system of growth, no longer corresponds to the contemporary rhythm of life. So now you no longer have to give up the physical body, you no longer have to waste time with all these transformations, you can in this very body, learn to reach higher states of consciousness, with the help of special methods and, with this very body, ensure your spiritual growth. And as for those who have already left,

well, you have to bring them back, through the procedure of resurrection.

I would like to point out that always – both before and now – there have been people capable of living as long as they see fit. They belong to that category of people who understand and know from personal experience what authentic consciousness is.

For this reason, in particular, these people understand that life is a simpler, a more accessible and natural reality, and that it is achieved by developing Consciousness.

4. Energetic Plane: In accordance with the principles and methods described in this book we can completely modify our lives. We have already discussed the possibilities of avoiding total earthquakes and

other catastrophes, building completely new spaceships, creating planes capable of flying, resuscitating, and rebuilding human organs. There are already some proprietary devices that carry this out thought control. I also developed new energy sources, which will allow you to completely defeat nuclear power plants and solve the energy problem once and for all. The new sources of energy allow it to be produced without causing damage to the environment. We have already mentioned the possibility of obtaining it for example from the time of past events.

Let's add another example of building teams of the future. Based on the principles proposed by me, the supercomputer with infinite data processing speed and unlimited memory can be created. You can imagine that the size of the computer will have to increase a lot and its construction becomes more complicated. But this is not the case! My inventions show that a physical item can contain an infinite amount of information. So unlimited speed and unlimited memory can be realized on a small microprocessor.

5. Physical or material Plane: TIME AND SPACE DO NOT LIMIT THE DURATION OF THE USEFUL LIFE. THE CONCEPT OF USEFUL LIFE IS FORMED BY THE RELATION OF THE SPIRIT WITH SPACE AND TIME (2.3).

Space, like time, is a construction of consciousness. Space is the structure that serves to carry out the actions of both the soul, the spirit, the consciousness and the body. There is a space of the soul, a space of the spirit, a space of consciousness and a space of the body.

The space of the body is that space in which the body moves, that is, the common physical space.

The space of the soul is the organizing structure of the World.

The concept of physical space here can no longer be used. The soul space takes precedence over the other spaces.

We note that the space of the soul is a secondary concept with respect to the soul itself: the soul is the foundation, the base.
The soul exists in an "absolute space in which God created it." The spirit exists instead, in a space of action, and here the space is connected with the concept of consciousness.
When a person thinks about something, this happens in the space of thought.

The space can be both individual and common. Each person has an individual thought space, but when some people – for example, in a cinema – watch a movie together, then the thought space becomes common.

The way in which consciousness reacts to what happens has a fundamental significance, because consciousness can transform space, and also physical space. It is enough that the consciousness emits an impulse for action and the space changes.

SIXTH DAY AFTER BIRTH

Baby, you are an independent thinker.

You as an adult just focus on how the Baby will transmit knowledge and information to you and how he/she will talk to you about different situations.

SEVENTH DAY AFTER BIRTH

Baby, this seventh day of your birth is number 7, a special number and it is yours, it has been granted to you from heaven, where the Creator is, who has created everything. Your Mom and Dad were created by the Creator; how you will be as a creator and how you will create as well. Now it is important for you to understand how the Creator has created the number seven and how the World was created.

EIGHTH DAY AFTER BIRTH

I mentally convey to you, that you, my baby, are an element of Eternity. You are eternal and now. If we draw the number eight next to you, you will get eternity, and if you transfer the number eight to zero, you will be able to get the entire number line. In other words, you will have to learn to see the transformation of symbols through the mental transfer of information, and therefore you can also understand how the body is built through the combination of elements. That is, as soon as you feel that the number eight can be folded, then you will get a zero, and if you look at it from the side, from the number line, then you can see a doubled zero. So it turns out that you transferred all the elements to zero and received the image of the transformation of numbers, so you can receive the transformation of any matter to recreate yourself.

NINETH DAY AFTER BIRTH

Baby, you are an individual personality that unites all the elements of the World, and you create the World, and therefore you are unique.

(Praise the Baby in every possible way)

Baby, you are unique, you are very special, you are kind, gentle, loving, wonderful, you are very intelligent, you have developed your clairvoyance and you will be very, very happy.

TENTH DAY AFTER BIRTH

On this tenth day, do you remember the number eight that was transformed to zero? And after the transfer of number eight to zero, number one came out and moved to number one, which is you.

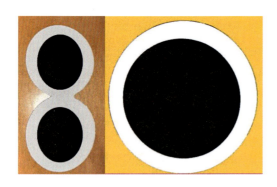

I will explain to you the basis of this principle and how the World is being born, how it arose:

FROM THE BOOK: RAPID DEVELOPMENT OF CLAIRVOYANCE CONTROL

With this method, when you study the structure of the creation of God by Himself, you simultaneously see how God created human Consciousness, considering precisely the technologies of the creation of Consciousness, Spirit, Soul. As I said, it is necessary to consider their creation from the physical body.

But at the same time, there is a certain mechanism of cognition of the whole World in its entirety, when man must fully understand, how the other elements of the World, the objects of the World, except man, are arranged.

Therefore, in order to simultaneously learn the principles and technologies of the creation of the Consciousness of other beings, in this action you need to see the World as God sees it, with the eyes of God. And then it will be possible to see how the Consciousness or the structure of the Consciousness of other living beings is also created.

I will also explain to you how all the connections of the World occur:

It is necessary to consider the principles, methods and structure of the creation of human Consciousness, the God-Creator of the whole World and of any other being, having Consciousness or a structure similar to human Consciousness.

In terms of the logic of the information exchange processes in the World, it is clear that God created precisely from the sphere of temporary absence. Moving now at this point along the temporal level of Consciousness, the point that is, before the moment of God's self-creation, it can be felt, and seen how the beam of light is organized from the physical body in this area, and this beam passes through certain

matrices of light matter. When working in the material, with these technologies that Dr. Grabovoi is giving, it is necessary to take into account that the information of the whole World is contemplated with the spiritual vision, with the vision of the Soul, and by the fact, which is contemplated, in terms of technology; information is not always connected to some logical cause and effect systems. Therefore, when you work simultaneously with others on the control, try to develop the same system of displaying information and events in the World. And be aware of it and how you can understand this based on the number.

ELEVENTH DAY AFTER BIRTH

(Mentally tell him):

Baby, use your mental vision and look around you, and recognize yourself as the creative personality that you are, and that helps mom and dad.

TWELFTH DAY AFTER BIRTH

(Do this exercise several times).

Lovingly tell her: *Baby, you are the best.*

And then mentally you also repeat to him several times: *"you are the best", "you are the best", "you are the best", "you are the best".*

THIRTEENTH DAY AFTER BIRTH

Allow the Baby to touch some things, place a doll in his/her hand, and other objects, (as many as possible).
You can also give things mentally; you can use other materials and put them in the baby's hands, and play with the Baby, saying two words: *"Yes, no. Yes, no."* (Repeat them more than ten times).

FOURTEENTH DAY AFTER BIRTH

(Massage the baby's feet) or Massage the baby visualizing his/her feet.
And watch how the baby reacts to the following sentence:

"Light, is the World."

If the baby reacts emotionally to the phrase: "Light, is the World," you need to observe the reaction at that moment, or throughout that day. To calm him down, read him some nursery rhymes, for example:

THE CHICKEN AND THE PIG

A fable for children about gratitude

A hen drinking
from a stream,
with each drink it raised up
to view Heaven,
and with its beak
gave thanks to whomever made
liquor so rich
What's that?
Grunted a pig
What does such a ridiculous grimace mean?

And she replies:
Nothing, neighbor.
Gratitude is Greek to a pig.
But there is no noble soul that does not thank
even a drop of water to be offered;
and even the chicken can
feel its inexhaustible
divine goodness.

Author: Rafael Pombo

THE NIGHT AND THE SNOW

Poem

Innocent moment
of tenderness and compassion,
my soul throbs of infinite joy,
and comforts my whole being.

Oh! Warm night,
fluffy white flakes
falling they go gently.
Tender images come to me
of love in all its splendor.

And I see how they go hand in hand
peace and unconditional love.
Soul, Spirit and Consciousness.
Delicate presences
of this world without end.
Just like you, they are eternal.
Oh, wonderful truth!
Oh, be infinite!
Feel this great love,
given to us by our Creator.

Author: Edilma Angel.

If the baby is calm, everything is fine.

See if the reaction is very different when you say:

Baby, "The World is Light"

If he does not show emotion to the phrase **"The World is light,"** in this case, you need to take action to achieve a certain level of mental arousal in the baby. Tell some stories, bright and unusual, for example:

All this can be felt by you. The child may not show any external signs. So, it will be your own opinion and criteria of how you feel or think that the baby has reacted. That is, we are already talking about the telepathic level of communication.

AN ELEPHANT WAS SWINGING	CU CU SANG THE FROG
An elephant was swinging on a spider web. As he saw that he did not fall She went to look for another elephant.	Cucu cucu Cucu cucu Cu cu sang the frog Cu cu under the water
Two elephants were swinging on a spider web. As they saw that they did not fall They went looking for another elephant.	Cu cu a gentleman passed by Cu cu with cape and hat Cu cu a lady passed by Cu cu with a tail suit
Three elephants were swinging on a spider web. As they saw that they did not fall They went to look for another elephant, ... (repeat with increasing numbers).	Cu cu a sailor passed by Cu cu cu selling rosemary Cu cu asked him for a bouquet Cu cu he did not want to give him any Cu cu and he began to cry
Author: James Locker	Author: Montserrat del Amo

Thus, I have provided you with the telepathic level of communication.

Now, concentrate from the first day of birth and in all the stages of your work with the baby, and say:

The Creator determined a task for you. The task is, that you must acquire knowledge and be a creator and you must work on this task, furthering yourself in your development with active movements. You must already try to speak, or use telepathy, or in some other way communicate even with actions to show what you want, and you can also speak logically.

FIFTEENTH DAY AFTER BIRTH

You can do this exercise mentally or through a drawing.

Baby, this is the letter "A"

(You can show the baby any other letter)

Baby, the first letter of the alphabet is A, there are also other letters, which have been created in order to facilitate communication. You can use them or you can also communicate telepathically.

Contacto con Grigori Grabovoi 3582295
Hacerle preguntas 417584217888
Ayuda telepática 14111963

GRIGORI GRABOVOI®

SIXTEENTH AFTER BIRTH

Baby, today I am going to talk to you about plants; There are different varieties, among which we find decorative plants, plants with wonderful flowers, fruit trees and vegetables, an excellent food source for your health. And animals like mammals, birds, etc., in the course of eternal life, will all exist infinitely, these conditions will be created on Earth.

SEVENTEENTH DAY AFTER BIRTH

Baby, the World is set and it is within a very large space.

The configuration of the World is infinite and the spaces are huge.

EIGHTEENTH AFTER BIRTH

Baby, as the World is very big, in order to travel you need to know the concept of time, that is, in the World, when you move from one place to another, or around the World, doing so will take time.

NINETEENTH DAY AFTER BIRTH

Baby, today your only task will be to ensure creation and therefore you must know exactly from now on what mechanisms of Creation you are going to master from this day on.

TWENTIETH DAY AFTER BIRTH

(Mentally focus on the first and second day after the birth of the Baby and along this axis, which I have drawn, and convey the sensations and memories, which were there on the first and second day).

From the first day of your birth, I remember when I transmitted to you the idea that the world is eternal, do you remember? And on the second day after your birth, I transmitted to you the idea that the World is eternal, and that the World at the same time changes, and that everything moves, while the World develops.

If you don't want to remind him of the details, then focus on the numbers:

One and two along this axis, and you transfer them, mentally, to this twentieth day.

If you don't want to remind him of the details, then focus on the numbers:

One and two along this axis, and you transfer them, mentally, to this twentieth day.

If you don't want to remind him of the details, then focus on the numbers one and two along this axis, and you transfer them, mentally, to this twentieth day.

This is how you work on the transfer of thoughts through the system.

....

Another action that you need to perform is going along the line drawn from the number twenty back along the vector to the first day after birth and immediately from there back to the number twenty.

TWENTY-FIRST DAY AFTER BIRTH

Baby, every element in the World is represented by some kind of schema. That is, the ray of light can have a shadow; a number can have a reflection; the mirror can have a reverse, or a number can be simply written or glued together and it will also have a shadow; but it will also be a number at the same time.

Do not simplify the task; you must explain exactly the way I said it.

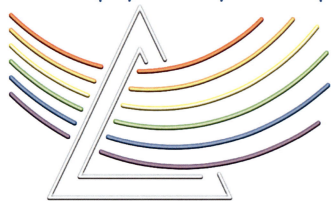

Try to explain it in great detail; quite a bit of time can be allotted to that, up to half an hour of continuous mental contact.

For example: if the number twenty-one is pasted and illuminated by a ray of light, it will also have a shadow, that is, not only the ray of light has a shadow, but it can also come from a number, and the number is a symbol, for example, of twenty-one objects.

And I explain to you, Baby, that all phenomena are related to each other, both symbolically and directly or without any symbolism.

TWENTY-SECOND DAY AFTER BIRTH

Baby, there are real connections behind the symbols, which often cannot be seen, after the symbol has been displayed, they are not visible.

(Observe if the baby understood it)

Baby, you must feel your own state of health, and cope with some feelings, with some possible deviations in your health. But I want to explain to you that you were created to always be healthy, and therefore you are already capable of facing any deviation from the norm, in your perfect health.

This is a persuasive conversation for anyone caring for a baby.

TWENTY-THIRD DAY AFTER BIRTH

Baby, you can already mentally communicate with other babies like you, whether they are twenty-three days old, boys or girls, even if they are in completely different areas of the planet, and even if they are at different times. You can contact all of them. Now I will teach you this specific practice.

Imagine yourself, feel that state of when you were twenty-three days young and try to join your baby at the telepathy level, that is, mentally imagine yourself, as a baby as if you were close of him or her, listening to him or her there, keeping him or her close.

Then you will feel how the baby communicates with you, and what language and symbols he uses, and these will become clearer to you. The language of your communication can be very varied, then you will be able to very quickly transmit all the creative knowledge that you have accumulated. Therefore, this is a very powerful day regarding the transfer of all the knowledge that you have accumulated; either instantly or as a boost, or with more detailed parts.

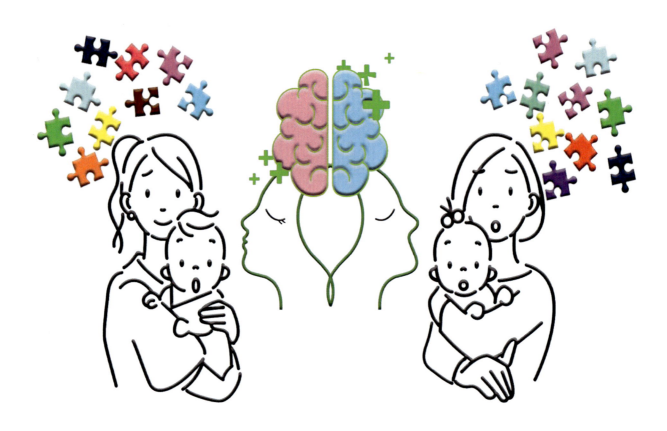

TWENTY-FOURTH AFTER BIRTH

Baby, I explain the following:

All numbers are united, and if you take any number, from this number you can get again a simpler number, for example, by adding or adding two plus four, and if you turn it over, you will receive the number nine. And like these examples you will find many more.

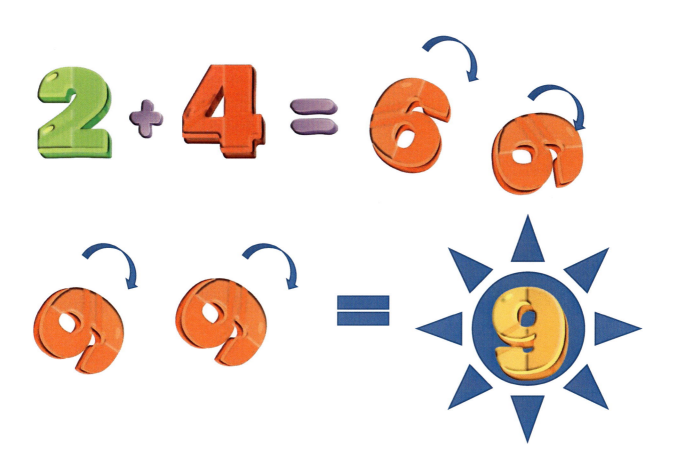

¿You see it?

TWENTY-FIFTH DAY AFTER BIRTH

(This is the training that should be carried out with the baby):

Baby, yesterday we flipped the two plus four, and it was upside down and that's how you got nine, which comes from flipping the two plus four, flipping it upside down, you got nine. But, it turns out that two plus five is seven.

 But if we have on the left side two plus four backwards

 is nine. And two plus five is seven,

that means we can subtract two from nine to get the number seven.

It is necessary to start performing these calculations mentally as I instruct you, in such a way that you can add numbers regardless of their locations. I mean, not in a logical way, but in the way that I have explained to you; rotating

the symbols, or in the form of comparison.

For example, if there is a number two. next to a four,

in principle we will have two plus two, which gives us four.

However, when placing two over two we get a mirror reflection,

And we can use this mirror reflection as a subtraction.

In other words, the child must learn to subtract, not what they are taught at school, but to subtract by combining the symbol with reality, that is, to work on reality immediately, but not on the symbolic basis, which is the reflection of reality. To explain it more precisely.

Baby, I'll give you another example: two plus four, turning around, (due to the physical twist that occurs in physical reality), gives a cut figure six, and we get a nine; two plus five is seven, and we can get that seven, if we put, two out of nine, the two that were in the number two plus four, in fact, should be two plus seven. So the four here played the role of the seven, if it hadn't turned around, but when we turned it upside down, then, it started to play the role of seven. In other

words, numbers can be added and transformed like this. And in this way you can develop your own systems; detailing the World, showing that the connections could be made more unusual, more colorful, and at that stage this is a great pleasure to develop.

This same type of work can be done with some objects, although they may be in different rooms.

For example: **Baby here is an object nearby, a television and your bed.**

Baby,

mentally put the TV in front of you, and now watch various programs. What you see on the screen is a symbol, and what you see on TV is reality. The mental transference is also a symbol, but you, through a symbolic transference, get the reality.

TWENTY-SIXTH DAY AFTER BIRTH

Baby, you are already an adult, now, visualize yourself in the future, already being an adult. Mentally observe yourself and you will see yourself as an adult and what you observe that happens there, in that future; you can improve any situation, to create what you want in the future.

You too can see where the baby has been looking, and if you see something out of the norm, you must repair it immediately so that everything is okay for him or her, there in the future, so that as an adult they have a life full of happiness.

TWENTY-SEVENTH DAY AFTER BIRTH

(Explain in the way you find most convenient).

Baby, on this day we are going to see the number nine again, but this time it does not need to be turned upside down or upside down, although we are going to combine it, if you add two to seven. Or if you overlap two and seven.

Do you see the number nine?

TWENTY-EIGHTH DAY AFTER BIRTH

Baby, today we are going to talk about your parents, there are connections in this existence that are biological and hereditary, you are also going to meet many people, some close to you who are called relatives, in the future you will have acquaintances and friends, with whom you are going to interact.

And in this way you should try to make the baby make as many sounds as possible and throughout the day, so that he communicates verbally, sings and plays actively with your baby.

TWENTY-NINTH AFTER BIRTH

Baby, your body is formed with eternal physical elements and a spiritual foundation, and that is all you need for eternal life. Now we are going to set the goal for you to develop eternally, based on the idea that "the World is eternal", this World was transferred to you during your first day of birth, and also that every moment, you can create a healthy body for yourself. let it be eternal.

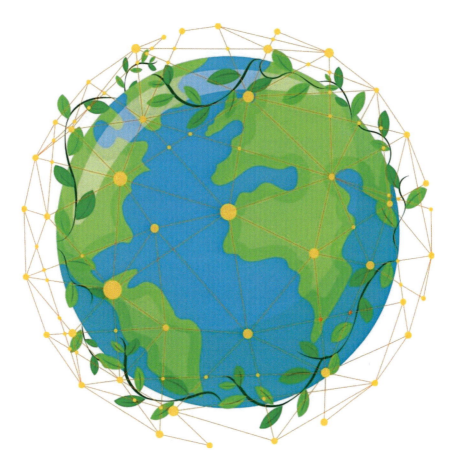

Grigori Grabovoi: All these actions can be performed on any person and at any stage of his life.

If you're doing it for yourself, you just have to mentally go in and imagine living those days and going through all the exercise until after your birth, then you do the same as you would with a newborn, and the same applies when you do it. You do for someone else, therefore it is clear that this system is done to restore physical health, yours or anyone else's.

THIRTIETH DAY AFTER BIRTH

(Try to engage the baby with more active, physical movements)

It is also possible to work mentally, and/or do physical massages.

Baby, I remind you that you must help your parents, and understand that in your development and growth you will have physical work, starting with learning to crawl and then walking; therefore, your task is to have a good physical development and be as active as possible, and something very important to understand is that you are infinite. In other words, develop yourself on the basis of infinite physical development.

THIRTY-FIRST DAY AFTER BIRTH

Baby, I'm going to share this with you; the World is arranged in a uniform and diverse way at the same time. This is an example, if you were to take a cube, a sphere, a plant, etc., they are separate elements that have different shapes, and inside each one there are other shapes, for example, inside a plant there are leaves, the cube it has sides, and if you join the sides, you would have two cubes with adjoining sides, and if they are attached, you would have a parallelepiped.

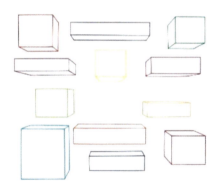

6 sided figures

And this is how many phenomena are created in the World, you now understand that they are very diverse phenomena.

Grigori Grabovoi contact 3582295
Ask question to him 417584217888
Telepathic help 14111963
GRIGORI GRABOVOI®

Grigori Grabovoi: What I said regarding each day of growth of the newborn, use the transference of telepathic thoughts each day and, consequently, you will create an individual development for the baby and your own methods.

***

The following information is for each month beginning on the day of birth. We're done with the first month, so I'll start with the second month, the third, etc., up to the twelfth month.

DURING THE SECOND MONTH

(Throughout the month, perform telepathic thought transference)

Baby, Light is made up of different shades of Light, if Light is combined, it may not get brighter because of it, you may just have different colors. By having data on the colors it is possible to give a specific color to each event. In this way, I transmit to you during this second month, the information about colors:

3 Primary Colors

They are those colors that cannot be obtained by mixing any other, so they are considered absolute, unique. By mixing the pigments of these colors you can get all the other colors.

Secondary Colors:

Made by mixing two of the primary colors in equal parts 50%: green, violet, orange

Intermediate colors: colors that are a mix of primary and secondary, thus obtaining the so-called intermediate colors, which, as their name indicates, are "in between" a primary and a secondary color or vice versa. And they are named with the colors that make-up their composition: yellow-green; orange-red; greenish blue; blue violet; red-violet ,and yellow-orange.

Tertiary Colors: tertiary shades are made by mixing equal parts of a primary and an adjacent secondary color. These are tertiary yellow (green+orange), tertiary red (orange+violet), and tertiary blue (green+violet).

These colors are the most abundant in nature and therefore the most used in painting, since the most exalted shine through them and those of medium intensity come to life.

Quaternary Colors:
They are those obtained by mixing the tertiaries together: tertiary red + tertiary yellow gives a neutralized orange, tertiary yellow + tertiary blue gives a very neutral green (olive green) and tertiary red + blue gives a neutral violet similar to that of plum.

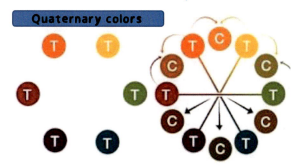

Colors also have features like Cold and Warm Colors.
These qualities are attributed to colors and are called "color-temperature."

The cold colors are all those that participate in the composition of blue and the warm ones are those that participate in the composition of red or yellow.

We associate warm colors (red, yellow, and orange) with sunlight, fire...etc. Hence they are classified as "hot." Cold colors are those that we associate with water, ice, moonlight...etc. (Blue and those that participate with it).

Note: information
https://www.tispain.com/2012/11/composicion-de-los-colores.html

From Grigory Grabovoi:
(from the book **"BUILDING MAN WITH LIGHT"**
In this theme I expose how to build the structure of man in terms of Light itself, through the transformation of Light. First of all, get the color and Light of the man in the control space, and then you will also be able to build, controlling the physical human body. And it will be possible for you to build a control structure by this method, in such a way that you will also be able to build the Light of your own activities. In fact, each next level of Light is the control in relation to the previous level, and vice versa. The above level, in fact, is also the level of mutual control. Light often possesses controlling isomorphic properties. The term "isomorphy" first designates a mathematical concept according to which when two structures can be superimposed in an isomorphic manner, each element of one structure corresponds to an element of the other, such that each one of the elements has the same role in its respective structure.

There is a type of universal control that goes from one level to another. For this, if you have control to infinity, if you consider the task in such a way - it means that you make the color infinite or the Light infinite. It also means that the infinite Light is still identified in the form of some local line in a control. It turns out that you carry out the control in the infinite environment, then you come to that Light, which manifests itself by a kind of larger mass in the infinite environment, and which is fixed in the form of some local segment.

If we consider the correlation, then each element of reality can be compared with the action of God: the infinite God is projected, for example, in the finite physical human body, in terms of size, in specific geometric shapes, and where the contact between God and man gives a new birth to color and Light, it is like a certain sparkle. So where does the primary Light usually come from? How is it initially perceived? It is the contact of God and man, the thought contact of God and the physical human body. The actions of God and the reality of God and the human physical body give birth, create a kind of spark, this Light, precisely, is the human understanding. The reality of God is a space of thought, which particularly contains the Pristine Light. And this Original Light is actually found in humans in a generative cycle. This generative cycle is how man is nourished from the inside.

When talking about a thought itself:
¿How is the thought itself, the action itself? Think, baby ¿how do these systems exist in the control space?
¿How does a thought move in general?
¿Where is it located? It is possible to perceive thought, in principle, in the form of a sphere in the form of Light. To consider driving mechanisms:
¿Why does thought move?
¿Why move in the information space?
It is possible to reveal this Primordial Light and illuminate yourself, or another person with this Light. This is how the physical human body can be built.

If we shine as the reverse of this Light, which is the Primordial Light within, and then there is another Light beyond some kind of thinking membrane, right? This is Light, which you have actually made due to the fact that you had your gaze beyond that membrane, which turns out to be the Light of your Soul. And here you can see very clearly the Light of the Soul, which has certain shades of bluish color, in this case, and it intersects with the Pristine Silver Light, which has some shades of bluish inside. That dark blue and bluish color tone (it is the transition/passage level) is the color giving birth to a form.

That is to say, when you transfer the form directly from the color of the soul, you can see, that it results in a form of a thought, in itself, a form of thought in itself, which is the primordial thing, in fact, it is like a human embryo. Therefore, a thought is born by analogy, like the very human embryo that begins to develop, and it turns out that the thought process is subordinated to the same process, in fact, like the birth of man in essence, precisely from the very beginning, and from the beginning of your organization.

It turns out that you can compare control levels of the same kind with what happens to man at a certain level of thought, for example, what you think will be the future. Therefore, in principle, if you put some thoughts on this axis of human development, from the embryo — see how man develops from this point. Therefore, we have to balance any point of information: for example, a human embryo, a thought, is a unified system of development. And it turns out to be the True Light, which relates to all people. The Light of Universal Divine Love, where love is a physical body. Therefore, it is possible to assign a segment right inside the body, directly in the tissue system, where the love of God is in a physical body, and it is clear that this is the body and you can't isolate a single segment. It's possible that if you would expand out a bit away from this level, you will see a healthy physical body. That is to say, where the love of God and man unite in a Harmonious Light, there will be your physical body, healthy, which is a little further from this level, but the infinite physical body is at the contact level of this Universal Love, so to speak, with man himself in his understanding, that's where we get to the root of thought, to the root of creation.

Baby, you can now orient yourself with this information and control it.

THROUGHOUT THE THIRD MONTH

(Transmit mentally to the baby)

Baby, all the parts of your body are connected, you have a head, trunk, arms, legs, and they are all connected to form a single body, and all the parts of your body are to be constantly developed, so your body will be indestructible.

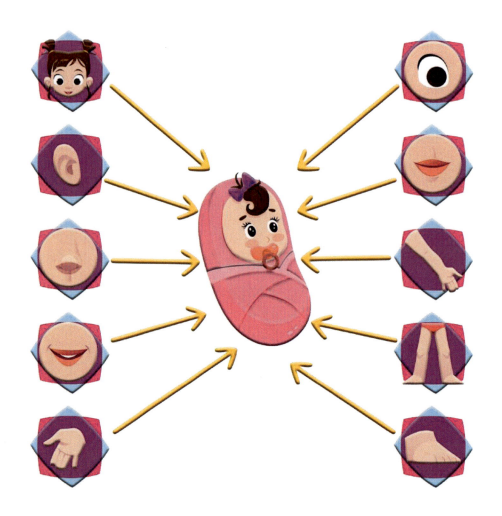

(Everything must be considered from your point of view).
The main thing here is to look, mentally at the baby's palms and mentally convey to him:

At this moment I take the palm of your hand, and your hand is in my thought, and now I transfer this thought of your hand to your thought. This exercise is for you to go to yourself, through your own thinking, then you will begin to develop your body towards infinity.

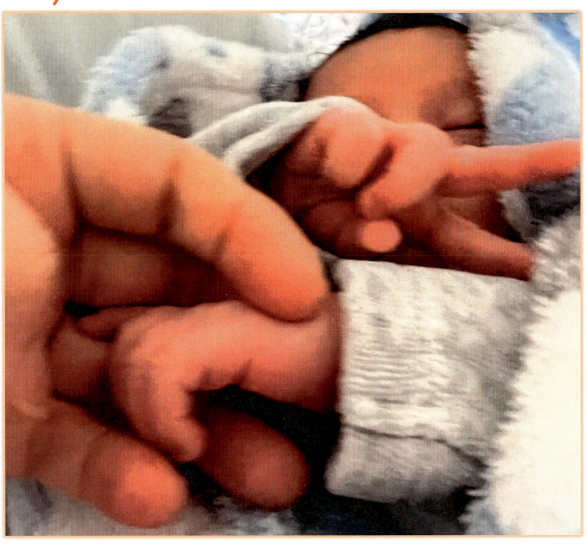

 ### THROUGHOUT THE FOURTH MONTH

(It is necessary to convey this data to him and try to explain it to him).

Baby, you are already able to walk, read, and write; you must do all this on your own. That is, you yourself should do it. And later, when others are going to teach you, you only have to compare it with what I am teaching you, and, from what is being taught, only correct what you have learned.

THROUGHOUT THE FIFTH MONTH

(The Baby needs to learn about the concept of infinite and finite, it is necessary to offer him this knowledge explain it mentally)

The infinite does not have and cannot have an end or limit. "The universe is infinite!" It is also numerous or very large, for example, by extending my arms to you, I show you that infinity is very large.

And the finite can be very small, has an end or limit in space or time, and therefore can be numbered or measured. Now bring your hands to a point.

Baby you must think this way mentally, each object consists of an infinite and finite part; the unification of these two parts results in the specific outline of an object. And you should even try to find, for example, in each object some infinite scheme and a finite one, and in this way I am going to explain writing to you, where you will find letters, whether vowels or consonants, that make up each word, and with the words become sentences.

(Or each element that you want to explain from this same position).

 ## THROUGHOUT THE SIXTH MONTH

(It is necessary to provide knowledge)

Baby, the development and movement of life is of infinite value, for the same reason the finite form manifests itself in the form of a body. That is, the body is the beginning of an infinite life.

Guide the child so that his/her education happens in continuous contact with you. And You should always feel the spiritual World of the Baby, try to make sure that the spiritual image of the World that the baby has is in harmony with the whole environment.

DURING THE SEVENTH MONTH

(Understanding)

Baby, today you will understand that all phenomena are connected, that when you eat you receive the energy from the food, and because of this you can walk; when you think you can receive and give energy or you can produce food. That is, you must be ready for the fact that the reception of food is a process related to your spirit, and this is provided by God, and at the same time this is Spirit, and this is provided by your parents. You must connect all this and have your own attitude, first of all; the attitude of harmony and the attitude of control, in relation to these connections.

When all these phenomena cause a good feeling, you are in a harmonious and loving feeling.

THROUGHOUT THE EIGHTH MONTH

EXPLAINING EVENTS

(This can be explained telepathically or with examples)

Baby when events happen in the World, these events are always related to you. For this reason it is necessary to consider the events that are taking place to harmonize them and to make them positive for everyone, that is, you can change them, remember that everything that happens outside of you is connected to you...

THROUGHOUT THE NINETH MONTH

(It is necessary to explain the origin of the letters and their sounds).

Baby, to describe the origin of the letters and their sounds; There are many theories about the origin of language. Many of these have traditional names and others are fun, like:

1. The Ma-Ma Theory: language could start with the easiest syllables related to more significant objects.

2. The Ta-Ta Theory: Sir Richard Paget, postulated that body movement preceded language, beginning with an unconscious vocal imitation of movements – just as a child's mouth moves when using scissors, or I clench my tongue between my teeth when playing the guitar.

3. The bow-wow theory: language begins as imitations of natural sounds — mu, chu-chu, pash, bzz, meow. It is better known by the name of onomatopoeia.

4. The Pu-Pu Theory: language starts with interjections, instinctive and emotional cries, such as OH! to indicate surprise, or OUCH! to indicate pain.

5. The Ding-Dong Theory: some people, including the famous linguist Max Muller, have argued that there is a mysterious correspondence between sounds and meanings. Words in English like "small," "sharp," and in general things that he calls "high," tend to have acute open vowels in many languages, while words like big and round, in general, things that he calls "low" tend to have closed back vowels. This is also known as sound symbolism.

6. The Yo-Hey-Ho Theory: language starting with rhythmic chants, perhaps eventually with the grunts of having worked hard. The linguist D. S. Diamond suggests that perhaps these were calls for support or cooperation accompanied by corresponding gestures. This could relate the theory to the Ding-Dong Theory.

7. The Sing-Song Theory: the Danish linguist, Jesperson suggested that language would have come out of play, laughter, cooing, courting, whispering, and similar emotional expressions. He even suggested that, contrary to theory, perhaps some of our first words were in fact long and musical, rather than short grunts, as others think.

8. The Hey You Theory: a linguist named Revesz suggested that we have always needed interpersonal contact, and that language began as sounds to signal both identity (here I am!) and belonging (I am with you!). We can also scream in fear, anger or pain (help me!). It is commonly called the contact theory.

9. The Hocus Pocus Theory: language may have had some roots in some sort of magical or religious aspect of our ancestors' lives. Perhaps we started by calling animals with magical sounds to tame them, which became their names.

10. The Eureka Theory: language was consciously invented, according to the Eureka Theory. Perhaps some ancestors had the idea of arbitrarily assigning sounds to mean certain things. Clearly, once the idea had been established, it would spread like wildfire!

Something else to consider is how many times language originated (or was invented). Perhaps it was invented once, by our earliest ancestors – perhaps by the first to have the necessary genetic and psychological properties to produce complex sounds and organize them into sequences. This is called monogenesis. Or maybe it was invented many times – polygenesis – by many people.

Perhaps the biggest debate amongst linguists and others interested in the origins of language is whether we can account for language using only the basic mechanisms of learning, or whether we need to postulate some kind of special formula for language.

Taken from Dr. C. George Boeree's Origins of Language (translated by: Claudio Fuenzalida).

At some point in human evolution, our ancestors went from making grunts to making more elaborate sounds, which gave rise to phonemes and words, and they had to choose a repertoire of vocalizations. so that each letter can denote a sound and each of the symbols can denote certain information. In other words, try to make sure that the baby understands where the information is presented in symbolic form and that the essence of the information can be both symbolic and real, but it is possible to control the meaning through the symbolic system, for example, write letters, then you get a word, and so on.

THROUGHOUT THE TENTH MONNTH

(It is necessary to show the child either through telepathy or on a physical level)

Baby, when you are looking ahead using your physical vision, you can also use longer distance vision beyond the physical, and see the same thing, but from another side.

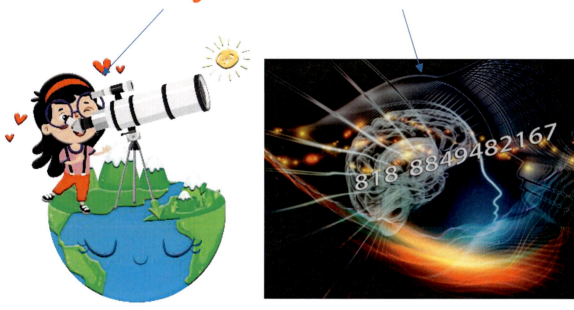

(In other words, you can actually mentally visualize that the baby is looking somewhere along a straight line and see as if he/she is facing you. Then you mentally show the baby what it is you would like to show the baby. This is already the development of clairvoyance.)

THROUGHOUT THE ELEVENTH MONTH

(Show forecast system)

Baby, this is the forecast control system, and when what you see from afar, moving towards you or away from you. These are the controllable forecast values. That is, you must understand that everything that you are considering in the World and everything that you can see ahead, and everything that you prepare to eat in the morning or watch a movie or study; all these phenomena are controllable and you can learn in advance how to do them better. In other words, tune them in a harmonious way, each day and look at them each day and the next in the future, and try to make them of maximum use to you and to each one with the intention and direction of saving the World, organizing your actions, mental and physical.

THROUGHOUT THE TWELVETH MONTH

(It is necessary to show the child an object, and for this, have a cube either painted on a sheet or physically)

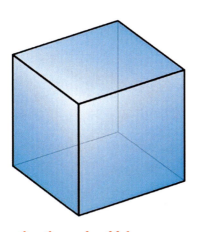 

Baby look at this example,
when you or we touch finite objects, on a physical level we can get infinite points. I'm going to show you, if we take this cube, we can touch its surface and now we're going to touch this point on the corner of the cube (and you put your finger there), and now look at my other hand that's touching the other side of the cube, and there you will see that there is a very small point, and it is so small that it can be infinitely small. That is, with this I want to show you that finite objects create infinities.

Grigori Grabovoi: *So far the baby is already a year old.*

- I will continue with periods for every year of life.

- This will be the first period of development of the child, which goes up to seven years of age.

- Then I considered other stages.

- The following methodologies will be developed for each year of the child's life.

DURANTE EL SEGUNDO ANO DE VIDA

(Education should be harmonious, not a formal explanation).

I want to show you my child that the World is infinite in the same way as vision. For example, now we are looking at the clouds, you see how the air moves them, there on the horizon, this is the vision, that you can see things that do not end and I also tell you that you can transfer your thought, and it can become infinite.

Finite contours contain infinite spaces. And further on is the infinity of your name, the infinity of your own thought, the infinity of your connections, the infinity of friendship, of love.

All these notions are related to the true infinity of the World.

There are connections that are infinite my love, and you will see that the infinity of the World gives rise to the infinity of love. The infinity of the World with all the stars and galaxies, gives rise to an infinity of relationships, and you will have a lot of goodness in your heart, and towards your parents, goodness with the World, with creation, well, and your creation in the World. You should also understand that this is even built on the basis of physical vision, for example, let's compare how it happens: if you look into the distance, the path ends there, but the horizon there converges, and you will see the horizon stretching from the sea, from the endless plain, and the finite gives way to the infinite at the point of convergence of physical vision. In the same way that thoughts can provide infinity at the point where they are finite.

DURING THE THIRD YEAR

(It is necessary to educate the child with respect to those around him)

I am going to explain how to correct those around you with love, since you are capable of stabilizing the attitude of the people who are close to you, and you are capable of spreading this attitude to everyone around you. That is, each person is involved in interpersonal relationships, well, each event is built according to certain laws. And your task my child is to control these events in such a way that everything is good for you and those involved.

For control you have to show him the following practice:

 My child, look, I am going to place my hand on a flat surface, or you can also see it in the air and now I extend my fingers, you can see that there is a distance between each finger.

Well, this distance represents all the events, and the fingers, for example, are all the people you know, see or remember, and if I put my other hand on the surface, the amount will increase several times and if dad puts his hand, it will be more quantity.

That is, my child, how many fingers can you imagine. So your task is to ensure that the distance between the fingers is good and suitable for the fingers to be comfortable, in other words, for all people to be comfortable and good, since all people are disposed to kindness and to develop creatively. In this way you will simply move your fingers and exercise control. And you can do it mentally, you don't even need to move your fingers, it is possible to transmit it mentally, without showing anything physically.

DURING THE FOURTH YEAR

(It is necessary to show him that there is feedback for each phenomenon)

My child, I am going to tell you about various phenomena that occur, for example, if a stone is thrown into the water, and it is a flat rock and it skips in the water in several places, it will create wave movements, ripples, and the waves overlap or join the other wave, and if the water forms waves and the rock jumps on the surface of the water several times, the contact with those waves could be at a different point than the sinking of the same rock. And those who are under the water, the fish, see it too, they will see that waves touch each other.

That is, there is feedback for each phenomenon, because the fish, once they saw the rock fall under the waves, swim away from the rock, and at that time the feedback is expressed, so that when the waves touch each other , the fish will see it too, and at the same time there are no fish near that rock.

(In other words, use this example to explain that there is a consequence for every event and teach control through consequences.)

My child, when there is some sign of an event at your disposal, you must understand that through that sign, you can trace it back to the original cause, for example:

¿Who has thrown the rock and how was it thrown?

And I want to tell you that this is called the development of predictive ability through clairvoyance, and by having the ability of clairvoyance, in the future, you will be able to have healing abilities.
That is, finding such connections will allow you to find the cause and eliminate the disease. Also, at this age it is possible and you can regenerate yourself and others.
Supporting and developing this capacity in other people as well.
And there is a mandatory element: you must mentally transfer this knowledge to others.

THROUGHOUT THE FIFTH YEAR

((It is necessary to explain to the child that the way the World works is when the whole World wants the development of the World.)

I am going to explain to you that the World works, when the whole World desires the development of the World, then the World will necessarily develop in this way, in a good and positive way; you too will wish for the creative and positive development of the World, think this way, for the World to develop creatively, then may your actions and desires encompass this; therefore it is necessary that you work on these methods of thought, that is, demonstrating how oneself can think, for example, having looked at oneself, in such a way that the whole World could be contiguous points, then simply by moving or being in a good mood in your Spirit, you will be able to control this World by moving it in a positive direction.

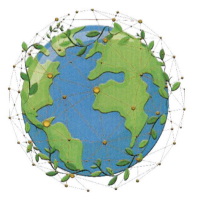

THROUGHOUT THE SIXTH YEAR

(It is necessary to give the child knowledge about when he goes somewhere.)

Now my child, I am going to give you this knowledge when you go somewhere to a meeting, to an event or you are with someone, when you are there or when you do something, keep in mind that all this happens in relation to the World that has already been created, and is being created, in relation to the Creator. And when these meetings take place, you must see, where is the manifestation of the Creator, where is the manifestation of the global image of the World, where is the fundamental, that is, the main level of the World that produces adult life, that is, the point where the transition from action and understanding of the World, is carried out in specific practice and takes place in the form of information. That is, you must understand that fundamental meaning of the World, and follow these specific actions.

THROUGHOUGHT THE SEVETH YEAR

(Transmit to the child, how the event is established from the point of view of the fundamental level of the World.)

I am going to explain how an event is established from the point of view of the fundamental level of the World. You must see very clearly and systematically: at a fundamental level the World can be explained like this; I am going to use very simple examples, for example, there is a tree, and the tree grows because it has a nutritious environment. And the nutritive environment is based on the fact that there is a soil. So we see that the ground is created, by the Creator. Everything that surrounds you is also created by the Creator, and you must understand how the Creator created everything, then The Creator has a system and you my child can have a system and for this you must understand the connections, and create how the Creator creates, so you can create and in the same way, and then everything will be correct. I know that you will develop at school, or while reading, and you will be able to develop any ability in harmony with the creative idea that the Creator establishes in the form of the creation of the World.

Now I will establish the second period of man's development, which is from eight years of age to fourteen years.

***

DURANTE LOS OCHO ANOS DE EDAD

(You must convey the knowledge in the form of a literature presentation, on a telepathic level.)

The World is arranged discretely, that is, each part of the World can be independent, and it is possible to find connections between the elements of the World, to obtain completely new solutions.
This is the beginning of the search for new solutions and it is very important to understand it in general terms, in this development it is always possible to go back, correct if there is something to correct and continue; in retrospect, telepathically you can also explain everything to anyone or a child even if they are at a distance, that is, anything you can do mentally, however, it is possible to do it also physically or simultaneously.

DURING THE NINE YEARS OF AGE

(It is necessary to give the child the mechanism of practices and specific tasks).

Now you will be able to connect all the phenomena of reality in the form of control, that is, the mechanism of specific practices, with a controlling structure being clear and precise, thus you will understand that the World is controllable; for example, when you speak, use harmonious and soft words. It's like modeling clay, which when modeling is given different shapes and you can use it in various ways and obtain different contours. That is the impression and the real action,

for you to achieve it, sometimes it is necessary to practice more with some accepted physical actions, others with some mental practices and tries to show that, from the point of view of the fundamental reflection of the World, it is you can do everything using Consciousness, and so it will not be necessary to do it physically.

DURING THE TEN YEARS OF AGE

(Teach the essence of combining the elements, related to living and existing nature, with other elements.)

Nature lives and is with other elements; in this case it is the essence of the combination of elements that should derive from the common goal between the types of elements: for example, a tree grows in order to provide oxygen for people, and also for people to walk and build on a piece of land firm, so that they grow their food and feed themselves. Therefore, the living tree generates oxygen and the soil also exists for the purpose of developing life. In principle everything is moving in the direction of expanding life, and I can prove it to you by showing you these drawings of practical and specific examples from daily experience; a child eating an apple, which comes from a tree that is planted, or children playing on a green meadow in a park, which was built on dry land.

DURING THE ELEVENTH YEAR OF AGE

(It is necessary to explain to the child that when he develops creatively and progressively, he is building for himself a stable systematic future).

When you develop creatively and progressively, you will be building for yourself a stable and systematic future, which adjusts to a system, and will be conditioned by the fact that development is always related to the accumulation of knowledge. To give you some exact examples: let's assume that you study some science, and by studying some subject, you will be able to work telepathically, and you can exercise control, and it will be true that creative activity will produce new horizons for creation. That is, only creation is the beginning of universal development, including your own development. You must not destroy anything.

THROUGHOUT THE TWELVETH YEAR OF LIFE

(It is necessary to show the child that, in fact, she/he is already an adult)

(Call her/him by her name) _____,

now it is necessary to tell you that you are an adult, you will see that things adjust to what you have received in knowledge during all this time. Looking at it from the point of view of the development of the things that have happened to you, and that already lead you to the adult state, and your previous development was not in any way different from the development that will occur now as an adult. I explain to you, at the age of twelve you have already accumulated a common point, where there is no disconnection between the previous age and the age now as an adult, in the future. That is to say, at twelve you must realize that you are the same as all the other creative elements of reality, and you have an infinite future, it will be light and happy for you, whatever you do you will do easily and with joy, everything will always be good for you.

Grigori Grabovoi: I am going to tell you the following:
To achieve the above, it is necessary that you congratulate the child more, give him many congratulations for all the things he does or says, give him gifts, go for a walk together and try to make the image of the World lighter.

THROUGHOUT THE THIRTEENTH YEAR OF LIFE

(We clearly explain the power of concentration)

Now you must clearly understand that by using intellectual concentration, you can concentrate properly; behave correctly at the level of thought, so you can control the world, control your reality. And for this, it is necessary to understand that this is exactly the right age to develop acceptable and feasible actions. I want to emphasize this fact and it is a truth: your thought changes reality and you must respond very clearly to it, all thought changes reality, so be sure and watch your thoughts so that your thoughts are quite accurate; treat your thoughts as a control mechanism.

THROUGHOUT THE FOURTEENTH YEAR

(Adulthood)

Well, now that your body is also changing and you see that you are really becoming an adult; in your fourteen years I ratify you and transmit this information: The World changes depending on your thinking: so the way you think is the way the Creator helps you in your development. In other words, feel your union connection with the Creator; feel it clearly and make an effort to see the coincidence of your actions, on the spiritual basis in union with the Creator, the action is that you can create how the Creator creates.

This third period is characterized by the fact that infinite future cycles are going to be used, adding the subsequent coefficient, simply with a number.

For example:

- If we are talking about the ages of 22 to 28 years: Then, it will be the same information that was used at 15 years of age, adding the concentration in number four. (Since it is the fourth period of development).

- If we are talking about the period from 29 years to 35 years: then, it will be the same information that was used at 15 years of age, adding the concentration in the number five (since it is the fifth period of development).

- If we are talking about the period from 36 years to 42 years: Then, it will be the same information that was used at 15 years of age, adding the concentration in the number six (since it is the sixth period of development).

- If we are talking from the age of 43 to 49 years: Then, it will be the same information that was used at 15 years of age, adding the concentration in the number seven (since it is the seventh development period) and so on.

THROUGHOUT THE FIFTEENTH YEAR

(It is important that the person perceives reality as a very specific and completely methodological control).

It is important that you perceive reality as a very specific and methodological control, with specific methods and generalized consequences. In other words, see that the specific is of a generalized nature, and from the general it is possible to reach the specific; It is important to understand that, from any small sign, it is possible to see an important consequence or an important past, how also in your fifteen years you must control the future in such a way that the future is arranged towards yourself).

THROUGHOUT THE SIXTEENTH YEAR

(Explain about time and space)

With the understanding of time and space from the point of view of data, which you had at twelve years, or even earlier, at three years of age; it is the beginning of life. That is, look at time and space as in a structure that is already familiar to you and to which you are already related. You are feeling the changes and the growth of your body, the growth of knowledge in your mind. This feeling serves as a platform for infinite development. At your sixteen years of age, observe the infinity of your development.

THROUGHOUT THE SEVENTEENTH YEAR

(Getting closer to the essence of God as the realization of the idea that life is eternal)

Observe how everything in your life has unfolded and these events are sequences that are determined by you, God, and you in conjunction with these events are a personality, a God-creator and you strive towards the Creator with your actions. This is the essence of God, the realization of the idea of man in eternal life, for this reason your actions must be thoughts; and through your actions of exaltation of life, you create eternal life; I explain more clearly: all your actions must be based on this technology and the application methods that you will use for control, must be quite specific, based on this specific practice that is now available to you, and to all the people who have it. It is necessary for you to do as much practice as possible for the realization of the events.

THROUGHOUT THE EIGHTEENTH YEAR

(Explain that when an event occurs, he or she is fully responsible for that event)

When any event occurs, you are responsible for that event. It is important that you now have a strengthening of your personal opinion and be sure to understand that in any case you are connected to the event at the level of common connections. And here it is necessary to develop your moral criterion, when you react to this event, from the point of view of common connections, you are a participant, a controlling self, and when this event concerns you personally, you feel it deeply. So from the depth of your Soul, and the depth of the Spirit, you must understand these specific events and control them based on the moral principles of control, which have the same levels of creation as life itself in human society.

THROUGHOUT THE NINETEENT YEAR

(We clearly know all future events at the level of our connections)

At this time, already at the level of your outings and the events that happen to you and depending on the objective in your life, you have already formed the ideology of your behavior. In other words, you must, do everything, keeping in mind a completely clear beacon and a very precise level of knowledge, which every human being possesses implicitly and intuitively, and sometimes evidently.

THROUGHOUT THE TWENTIETH YEAR

(Know and become aware that reality is always controllable)

No matter what events have happened to you, or have happened in society, reality can always be transformed in the way that each person wants. Make an effort and become aware of bringing the light, of bringing good, of using your intelligence and you can be calm, confident; when you stay in this position, you will always be ahead, you will always be winning, and you will always be successful and you will always be a beacon of light, for all those who follow the same line. In other words, a mutual movement forward and upward, towards the future to contribute to universal well-being and understand that you are entering the section of information on the development of people, and that they all depend on your actions.

THROUGHOUT THE TWENTY-FIRST YEAR

(A person must know that all the future must be realized within the timeline he/she set)

The infinite future has infinite periods; therefore, you should strive to achieve it technologically. In other words, this is the start year of the actions. You should know that it is the year in which you begin to act and it takes you to infinity, like every previous year you have built, but this year you move it along the path of infinity significantly faster. In this way, it is possible to increase the speed of adaptation of the Spirit to infinite development, concentrating on how to do it at twenty-one years of age.

About the following periods: actually, they are the same as the third period, that is, from fifteen to twenty-one years of age. The only and necessary thing is the concentration in each period respectively, with the number denoting the period.

- If we are talking from the age of twenty-two to 28 years: Then, it will be the same information that was used at fifteen years of age, adding the concentration in number four. (Since it is the fourth period of development)

- If we are talking from twenty-nine years to thirty-five years: Then, it will be the same information that was used at fifteen years of age, adding the concentration in the number five. (Since it is the fifth period of development)

- If we are talking from thirty-six years to forty-two years: Then, it will be the same information that was used at fifteen years of age, adding the concentration in the number six. (Since it is the sixth period of development)

- If we are talking from the age of forty-three to forty-nine years: Then, it will be the same information that was used at fifteen years of age, adding the concentration in the number seven. (Since it is the seventh development period) And so on.

THIS IS A TYPE OF INFINITE SYSTEM

Therefore, it is possible to develop it infinitely according to this number-based concentration system. Although this number-based concentration system has another special aspect; when you concentrate on the same number, it is still possible to make the numbers more varied: that is, the numbers can be added, four can be turned into two plus two, five can be turned into two plus three, and then perform the concentration through any of these numbers. Then other semantic nuances are visible.

How to receive semantic nuances, or guidance through the number?

The principle here is very simple. For example, focus on the methodology, which I provided at the age of fifteen, although you can and consequently do, receive completely new methodologies by breaking the number, for example, the fourth period, is identified with the number four. During concentration on the number four you have a fourfold increase, a fourfold amplification, etc. That is, each number can be used as an amplification, or as an expansion, or as a detailed four, so it is possible to do everything the same, but by assigning some semantic forms to the number.

Therefore, teaching at this level, for this cycle of education can be done for anyone, at any age, mentally transfer this education either to yourself, or to any other person, and thus develop the structure of any person and by doing so

restore or develop yourself spiritually and even cure diseases, and thus the future is improved.

IN OTHER WORDS, THIS IS REALITY BASED EDUCATION. THIS IS A UNIVERSAL CONTROL SYSTEM, WHICH CAN BE USED DIRECTLY, THAT IS, YOU SHOULD CONSIDER THE CONNECTIONS IN SUCH A WAY THAT THESE CONNECTIONS WILL BRING YOU SPECIFIC RESULTS IN REAL TIME.

For example, if a person wants to study according to my education system, it can be done in real time and at any age, in fact, it is possible to optimize the future in this way.

Who can do it:

- You

- An eighteen-year-old person, for example, who can do it for herself/himself, applying this teaching from the state that precedes birth, from negative infinity to positive infinity

- You can apply it to anyone, and always do it from negative infinity to positive infinity, and support others such as relatives, parents, grandparents, or children or young people, friends, or any elderly person, etc., it works in real time.

- And also all pepole can do it at any level, and in each year, apply these principles and develop the methodology on their own

In a practical case, if, for example: it is necessary for you to quickly learn a foreign language, or it is necessary for you to receive education in accordance with the harmony of the World and in accordance with the creation of the World, in order to understand and review the past education according to the fundamental laws of the World, use this system, adapting it to the knowledge you already have, or using the knowledge, or selecting something unique, or simply using an education system that works, etc.

In other words, to have a well-developed spirit, and to have the ability to receive information and be in control, you don't need to use books to study. It is possible to study independently and have all the answers, all the symbols, that is, it is possible to know how to move forward, and have the possibility of making materializations that will allow you to obtain everything, even the already written tests. Therefore, what is implied by education here is the kind of education where the Soul can build around itself the required sequence of events, and these events are also oriented towards the state of the Soul itself.

Also, this system of education can be used to treat diseases, for example, by understanding that if in some system harmonious connections were not taken into account, that is, the fundamental nature of the organization

of knowledge or actions, then as part of educational improvement giving information to cells, everything can change. In other words, if there is any disease. Through an explanation of this system, and through telepathic transference to another person or to oneself, it is possible to recover from illnesses.

Therefore, if we are talking about events, it is possible to improve the event through the harmonization of your own imagination, your views regarding the World, to your development, therefore your own development in this case will serve as control criteria. And normalizing your own development will give you adequate control even if you don't later perform specific technological actions to get a result.

For example, if you have to pass a test, or perform some action, or prepare for an event, then you can act on the event exactly, and thus obtain it's good, or simply bring it to the harmonious norm, that is, in harmony with the surrounding World through education according to the system that I have now taught you. Therefore, your event will be positive for you, in any case. In other words, that is why the formation of events, including the restoration of your own health, or the restoration of the health of others is the correct orientation in the World of information, the correct understanding of the laws of the World, the correct understanding of the laws of the Universe, and this education provides you with the ability to have that understanding, providing you with a capacity for original knowledge in terms of:

- ¿Why is the world organized this way?
- ¿Why do things happen this way in the World?
- ¿Why are the events connected to each other in this way?
- ¿Why aren't they organized differently?

And it makes it possible for you to find new connections and develop your own connections, your own methodologies and systems of salvation, and advance along the infinite path of eternal life in the physical World, which is also in the spiritual World, in the moral World, and which will arise during the application of these special moral laws of education.

Grigori Grabovoi

Development	514328 814975168
Prenatal development	491798679481
Mental development	949517398641
Thinking verbal-logical	8 528 9888 418 704
Love (emotion)	888 412 1289018
Love (eternal)	888 912 818848
Children (age development)	59148901739 8
Children (motor development)	591 489 016 7
Childhood	489067 319227
Child assertion	52861971819
Gifted children	489761 398063
Early talent (gift)	14 31988 317
Self-improvement	318719 819
Self-transcendence	9148142
Human awareness	819497264188
Progress	3917218949181
Action (primary)	519489 68 998
Homeostasis (organism)	498716 319 816
Soul	598061 291319 88
Eternal life	917532178919319
Global salvation	319817318
Biological clock	817498 8612194
Human	518849889814981
Human biotype	8193179148891497
Constitution	8184194851648198
Color perception	379 612 89047
Harmony	10^{17}

Made in United States
North Haven, CT
15 February 2024

48800622R00080